This book is an expression of love and frie

ALL KNOWLEDGE, THE TOTALITY
OF ALL QUESTIONS AND ANSWERS,
IS CONTAINED IN THE DOG.

— FRANZ KAFKA

CREDITS:
"OSCAR TAKES LARRY TO THE MOON"
REPRINTED WITH KIND PERMISSION FROM ROBYN MCDANIELS.

"THE BEST INVESTMENT..." FROM *DOG ENCYCLOPEDIA*,
USED WITH PERMISSION OF WILL JUDY, JUDY PUBLISHING.

"I KNOW LOVE..." FROM *DOGS* BY BETH BROWN.
USED WITH PERMISSION OF LION BOOKS, SCARSDALE, NEW YORK.

EFFORTS HAVE BEEN MADE TO FIND THE
COPYRIGHT HOLDERS OF MATERIAL USED IN THIS PUBLICATION.
WE WILL BE PLEASED TO INCLUDE THE APPROPRIATE
ACKNOWLEDGMENTS IN FUTURE EDITIONS.
SINCERE APOLOGIES FOR ANY OMISSIONS OR ERRORS.

10 9 8 7 6 5 4 3 2 1

ISBN: 0-8118-2292-3

PRINTED IN HONG KONG

DISTRIBUTED IN CANADA BY
RAINCOAST BOOKS
8680 CAMBIE STREET
VANCOUVER, B.C. V6P 6M9

CHRONICLE BOOKS
85 SECOND STREET
SAN FRANCISCO, CA 94105
WWW.CHRONICLEBOOKS.COM

He is your friend, your partner,
your defender, your dog.
You are his life, his love, his leader.
He will be yours, faithful and true,
to the last beat of his heart.
You owe it to him to be worthy of such devotion.
— Unknown

For Giorgia, my light,
and Sugar, the one-eyed Wonder Dog.

In memory of James Edward Sampson,
a true connoisseur of canines and all things.

♥

I KNOW LOVE.
I HAD A DOG.
— BETH BROWN

. . . A friendship that never betrays, a love that never cools,
a loyalty that knows no end . . . Every home needs a dog . . .
To grow up without knowing the love, companionship and
loyalty of a dog is to miss something out of life.
The old and the young alike, the rich and the poor,
the learned and the ignorant, the famous and the infamous,
the priest and the criminal, alike can benefit vastly through
the ownership of a dog and the companionship this ownership
brings. The world's best investment is that in a dog.

— Will Judy

FIRST IMPRESSIONS

WHERE WE MET & WHEN

_____

_____

_____

_____

_____

_____

HOW WE FOUND EACH OTHER

_____

_____

_____

_____

PUPPY TALES

NEAR AND DEAR
OUR FAMILY CIRCLE

_____

_____

_____

_____

_____

_____

_____

BEST FRIENDS

I'm a lean dog, a keen dog,
a wild dog and alone;
I'm a rough Dog, a tough dog,
hunting on my own;
I'm a bad dog, a mad dog,
teasing silly sheep;
I love to sit and bay at the moon,
to keep fat souls from sleep.

— Irene Macleod

GOOD DOG

NOT-SO-GOOD DOG

MY LITTLE DOG,
A HEARTBEAT
AT MY FEET.

— EDITH WHARTON

ENDEARING HABITS

_____

_____

_____

_____

_____

_____

_____

THE GREAT PLEASURE OF A DOG IS THAT YOU MAY
MAKE A FOOL OF YOURSELF WITH HIM AND NOT
ONLY WILL HE NOT SCOLD YOU, HE WILL MAKE
A FOOL OF HIMSELF TOO.

— SAMUEL BUTLER

Party Tricks & Special Talents

_____

_____

_____

_____

_____

_____

_____

_____

Celebrations & Special Occasions

_____

_____

_____

_____

_____

_____

_____

WHEN YOU FEEL DOG TIRED AT NIGHT,
IT MAY BE BECAUSE YOU'VE GROWLED ALL DAY LONG.
— UNKNOWN

To you, it is just a walk—twenty absentminded minutes between waking and coffee. But to me, it is a paradigm for our complex alliance— an elaborate dance of manners.

— Dylan Schaffer
on behalf of Sigourney (dog)

You will always be lucky if you know
how to make friends with strange dogs.

— Colonial American proverb

TRAVELS & ADVENTURES

_____

_____

_____

_____

_____

_____

_____

EVERY DOG MUST
HAVE HIS DAY.
— JONATHAN SWIFT

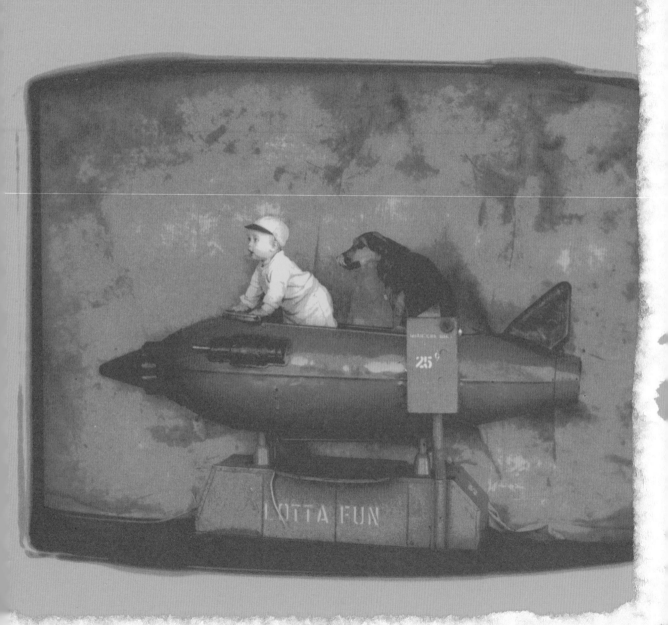

ALL IN TOWN WERE STILL ASLEEP,
WHEN THE SUN CAME UP
    WITH A SHOUT AND LEAP.
IN THE LONELY STREETS UNSEEN BY MAN,
    A LITTLE DOG DANCED.
AND THE DAY BEGAN . . .

— RUPERT BROOKE

LAST BUT NOT LEAST . . .

_____

_____

_____

_____

_____

_____

_____